Going Wild in Woolly Bush

For Howard and all the
Carry On films we watched

First published in the United Kingdom in 2021 by
Portico
43 Great Ormond Street
London
WC1N 3HZ

An imprint of Pavilion Books Company Ltd

ISBN 978-1-91162-259-8

A CIP catalogue record for this book is available
from the British Library.

10 9 8 7 6 5 4 3 2 1

Reproduction by Rival Colour Ltd.
Printed and bound by Toppan Printing Co., Ltd.

www.pavilionbooks.com

Publisher: Helen Lewis
Commissioning editor: Sophie Allen
Designer: Alice Kennedy-Owen
Set photography: Ed Hartwell
Cut out photography: Martin Norris
Master knitter: Caroline Bletsis
Additional knitting: Michelle Green and Sally Bentham

Going Wild in Woolly Bush

Bernard and Barbara's guide to getting it all out in the open

Sarah Simi

PORTICO nudinits

Deep in the heart of Woollenshire lies the village of Woolly Bush and in a cottage called Dunittin' live Bernard and Barbara. Together with the other villagers, like Jim the farmer and their local vicar, they go about their daily business of rambling, gardening, going to the pub and playing cricket — so nothing unusual.

Oh except they're all in the nudie and there's a very large innuendo waiting around every corner.

5

Bernard was pleased Barbara had

got her fondant fancies out

Barbara couldn't wait for

a stiff one going down

Barbara had mounted

Bernard's big one

BERNARD'S BIG ONE

Bernard's balls were

definitely out

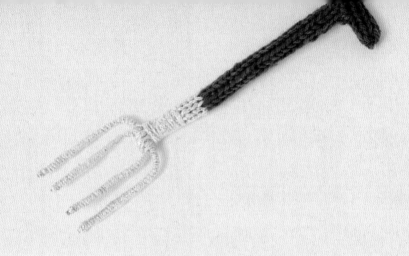

Bernard was struggling with a large upright

The vicar wanted a good go at

Barbara's Bushy Mound

Bernard had burnt his sausage

Bernard had brought Barbara to the summit

The vicar had never seen so much

wildlife around his nuts

All the men held their

wood in position

Bernard was trying to get it up quickly

Bernard had lost his dibber

in Barbara's clematis

The vicar had finally got a

clear view of the peaks

Bernard was really giving

Barbara the willies

Barbara's lobelia was showing well

Jim was having to

hold on very tight

to his Willie

Bernard had a good view of Bushy Mound

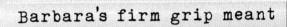

Barbara's firm grip meant

she got extra length

Bernard was impressed with

Barbara's blowing technique

Jim's Willie was always

lively on a windy day

Bernard liked the way Barbara

could handle a large chopper

Barbara was delighted to finally touch a menhir

Jim's cock was out in front

50

The wind had caught Barbara's flaps

Bernard was

definitely all out

Bernard was feeling rather stiff

Barbara was worried Jim

would burn his cheeks

Bernard had spent the morning pricking out

Bernard had lost his wood

Jim was having

trouble getting his

Willie over the stile

Bernard was very proud of his morning glory

The vicar had seen a

lovely pair of hooters

Barbara was surprised her box had been entered so soon

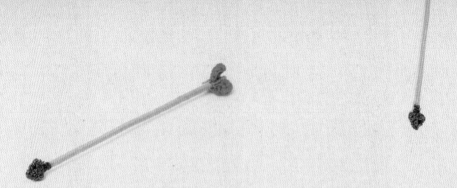

Bernard had finally got it in the bullseye

Bernard was about to get his

hands on a lovely pair

Barbara always thought

Bernard's sausage tasted

better outdoors

Try Rock Climbing!

GO DEEPER INTO BUSHY GORGE

- How to get to the peak quicker than your partner!
- Jugs - when are they too much of a handful?

Go Cave Diving!

- Explore the damper regions of Woolly Hole Cave

- Squeezing into a tight hole with all th right apparatus

- Need to buddy up to go down for the first time? We'll show you how

- Get up close to the famous 'Unsheathed sword' stalagmite

White Water Rapid Fun!

- Learn the correct technique for gripping your shaft

- Perfect for thrill seekers wanting a good rafting

IT'S HARD AND FAST!

Woolly Bush Tennis Lessons

inding just the ight lob

ightening your head
or **maximum** playing
leasure

echniques for getting it in
n the **first attempt**

Jew balls please!- know when
your balls are tired

Taught by ex-professional
**Wimblebum champion
Rod Shaver**

*Book your first
lesson today!*

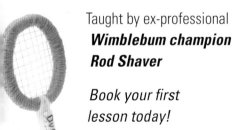

COCK FANCIER MAGAZINE

– Preparing your cock
for a show – tips from
Best in Show winner Jim
McFurry

– Is your cock always
up first thing? Ways
to keep your cock and
your neighbours happy

– Is having a large wattle
always a good thing?